Rules

by Margie Burton, Cathy French, and Tammy Jones

I follow rules every day.
The rules tell me what I can do
and what I cannot do.

Some rules keep me safe.
When I walk to school,
I look both ways before
I cross the street.
I walk. I do not run.

I wear my life vest when we go for a ride in the boat.

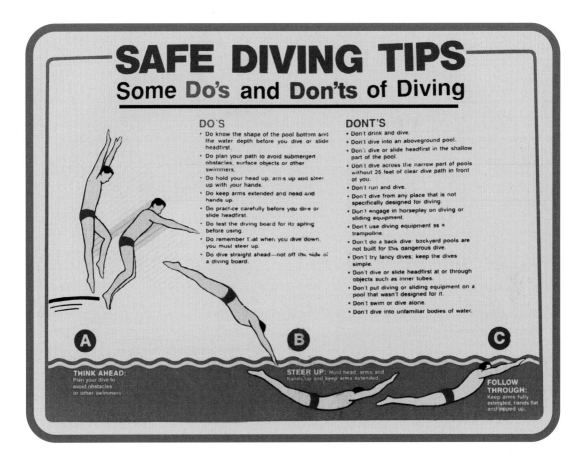

SAFE DIVING TIPS
Some Do's and Don'ts of Diving

DO'S

- Do know the shape of the pool bottom and the water depth before you dive or slide headfirst.
- Do plan your path to avoid submerged obstacles, surface objects or other swimmers.
- Do hold your head up, arms up and steer up with your hands.
- Do keep arms extended and head and hands up.
- Do practice carefully before you dive or slide headfirst.
- Do test the diving board for its spring before using.
- Do remember that when you dive down, you must steer up.
- Do dive straight ahead—not off the side of a diving board.

DONT'S

- Don't drink and dive.
- Don't dive into an aboveground pool.
- Don't dive or slide headfirst in the shallow part of the pool.
- Don't dive across the narrow part of pools without 25 feet of clear dive path in front of you.
- Don't run and dive.
- Don't dive from any place that is not specifically designed for diving.
- Don't engage in horseplay on diving or sliding equipment.
- Don't use diving equipment as a trampoline.
- Don't do a back dive: backyard pools are not built for this dangerous dive.
- Don't try fancy dives: keep the dives simple.
- Don't dive or slide headfirst at or through objects such as inner tubes.
- Don't put diving or sliding equipment on a pool that wasn't designed for it.
- Don't swim or dive alone.
- Don't dive into unfamiliar bodies of water.

A THINK AHEAD: Plan your dive to avoid obstacles or other swimmers

B STEER UP: Hold head, arms and hands up and keep arms extended.

C FOLLOW THROUGH: Keep arms fully extended, hands flat and tipped up.

At the pool I do not dive
from the side.

My dad follows rules, too.
He wears a helmet
when he is at work.
He wants to be safe.

My mom stops the car
when the light is red.
She is being safe.

Some rules keep me well.

I wash my hands before I eat.

This keeps me from getting sick.

I brush my teeth after I eat.

This keeps my teeth clean.

At school I follow the rules.
When I want to talk,
I raise my hand. I wait
for the teacher to call on me.

My friends and I take turns
on the playground.
We have so much fun when we
play by the rules.

After lunch, I put my leftover
food in the garbage can
to help keep our school nice
and clean.

I also work very hard at school
to get all of my work done.
School rules make it easy for
me to learn.

At home, Mom and Dad teach me the rules.

I follow the rules at the table when we are eating.

I use good manners.

I follow the rules
for doing work
and having fun at home.
These rules help my family
get along.

Do you follow this rule, too?

Wear your seatbelt
when you ride
in the car.